TUDOR AND STUART LIFE

Contents

Tudor and Stuart Times	2
The land of Britain	4
Life in the Country	6
The gentry	6
A rich man's house	8
Yeomen	10
Husbandmen	11
Farmworkers	12
Women	13
Life in the Town	14
Where were the towns?	14
Merchants	16
Merchants' houses	17
Shops and workshops	18
In the street	19
William Shakespeare and the theatre	20
Life at Court	22
Kings and queens	22
Courtiers	24
Royal palaces	26

Religious Life	28
Going to church	28
Roman Catholics	30
Protestants	31
Puritans	32
Witchcraft	33
Life in the Army	34
Civil War soldiers	36
The New Model Army	37
Life at Sea	38
The *Mary Rose*	38
Exploration	40
A New Life	42
India	42
America	44
The *Mayflower*	46
Index	49

Tudor and Stuart Times

Two powerful families, the Tudors and the Stuarts ruled for most of the sixteenth and seventeenth centuries. This is why these years are usually called Tudor and Stuart times.

These were all rulers in the Tudor family.
The Tudors ruled England, Wales and Ireland.
Which Tudor ruled the longest?

Tudors	
Henry VII	1485-1509
Henry VIII	1509-1547
Edward VI	1547-1553
Mary I	1553-1558
Elizabeth I	1558-1603

At the time of the Tudors, the Stuarts ruled Scotland. After 1603 the Stuarts ruled England, Wales and Ireland too.
These were rulers in the Stuart family.

Early Stuarts	
James VI of Scotland and I of England	1603-1625
Charles I	1625-1649

There was no king or queen between 1649 and 1660.
This was because Britain was a Republic during those years.

The Republic	
Britain ruled by a Council of State	1649-1653
Oliver Cromwell, Lord Protector	1653-1658
Richard Cromwell, Lord Protector	1658-1659

These were also Stuart rulers. They ruled Britain after the Republic had ended.

Late Stuarts	
Charles II	1660-1685
James VII of Scotland and II of England	1685-1688
Mary II and her husband William III	1689-1702
Anne	1702-1714

Republic
A country without a king or queen whose rulers are chosen by the people.

Tudor and Stuart Times

In this book you can read about the lives of many different people who lived in Tudor and Stuart times, and how their lives changed. Some even decided to make a new life in another part of the world.

This picture shows women washing clothes in Tudor times.

It helps answer some of our questions about the work ordinary people did, where they lived, the clothes they wore and the technology they used.

Only a few people took part in the big events, like the defeat of the Spanish Armada.

You can read about events and famous people in the book *Tudor and Stuart Chronicle*.

In this picture the Spanish Armada is being set alight by the English ships outside Calais.

Roman Numbers

Roman numbers are usually used when talking about kings and queens.

V means five and I means one. Henry VII is Henry the seventh. Can you work out what the rest of the kings and queens should be called?

The land of Britain

If we could travel back in time to when the first Tudor was king, what sort of place would we find?

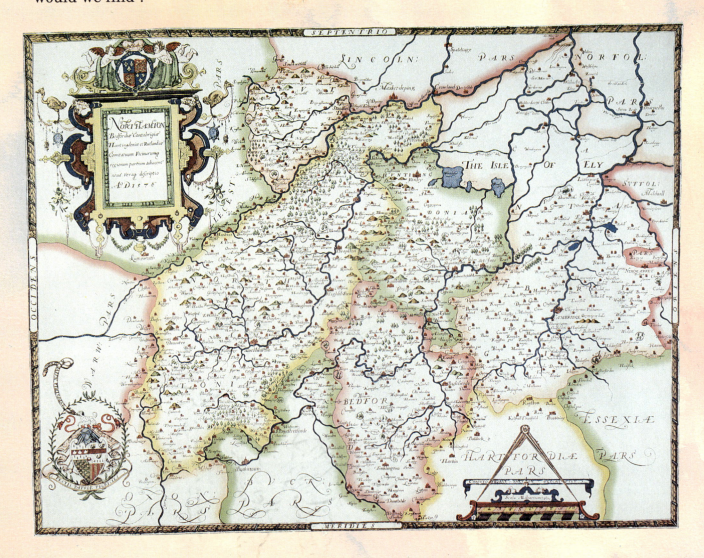

This map was drawn in 1576 by Christopher Saxton, a mapmaker who travelled all over England.

In his time most of Britain was countryside. We can see where there were patches of woodland and where there were hills, marshes and heathland from the pictures he drew on the map. Many of the villages marked on the map are still there today. But there is one big difference between this map and a modern map. Can you see what it is?

In Saxton's time the easiest way to travel was by boat on the rivers because there were no good roads. So Christopher Saxton drew rivers instead of roads on his maps because they were so important.

Tudor and Stuart Times

Much of Britain was covered in forests. Ancient oak and chestnut trees grew in the forests.

Some parts of the forests have survived until today, but they are much smaller now than they were in Tudor and Stuart times. The New Forest in Hampshire, Epping Forest near London, Sherwood Forest in Nottinghamshire, the Forest of Dean in Gloucestershire and the Forest of Arden in Warwickshire are some that we can still visit today. Wild pigs and deer, as well as foxes, rabbits, squirrels, hare and other small animals lived there. What has this traveller caught for his supper?

Between the forests was good farmland where sheep and cattle grazed, providing wool, milk and meat. In the fields, wheat, barley and beans were grown.

One German visitor to Britain at the beginning of the sixteenth century wrote about what a rich and fertile land it was. Even the rivers and ponds were full of fish and wild ducks which people caught for food.

Life in the Country

The gentry

Three quarters of the population lived in the country and worked in farming. The richest people owned land and were called the **gentry**. This needlework picture was finished in 1600 by women from the gentry. It shows some of the people, buildings and animals they saw every day.

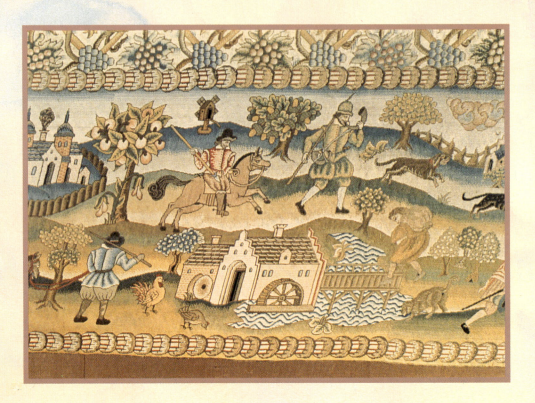

Find:
- a windmill.
- trees. What sort are they?
- a hunting scene. One huntsman is blowing his horn and the other has a pole with a knife on the end. He is looking for a wild pig.
- a farmworker with a sack of corn on his back.
- a water mill with a waterwheel and a grinding stone.
- a chicken and a turkey. What are they hoping to pick up outside the mill?

Gentry
They owned most of the land and were sometimes called 'country gentlemen' or 'landlords'. They paid the workers wages from the profits they made on the land.

Life in the Country

In Tudor and Stuart times landowners started to use their land in new ways and grew rich. They cleared parts of the forest and sold off the wood to build houses and ships. They found that they could make good profits from wool or corn by selling it at market. They stopped ordinary workers using small strips of land where they grew their own food, and even fenced off **common land** so they could keep more sheep or grow more corn to sell.

But the farmworkers grew poor. They had nowhere to grow their own food, put their pigs or sheep, collect firewood or pick nuts and berries.

Look at this picture of Sir Henry Tichborne, a rich landowner. It was painted outside his new country house in 1670. He was so rich that everyone else in the village depended on him.

Find:
- Sir Henry.
- his family. You will recognise the gentry from their expensive clothes.
- his servants wearing a uniform.
- the other people who live in the village. They are all going to be given some bread. Can you see it in the baskets and in the apron of the small girl at the front of the picture?

Common land

Land that was meant to be shared by everyone in the village.

A rich man's house

One way to find out about how the rich lived is to read a list of the things they owned when they died. The list is called an 'inventory'. Sir Anthony Drury, from Norfolk, died in 1638. There were thirty-seven rooms in his house altogether.

Some of the words used in 1638 are different from those we use, but we can understand what most of them mean if we read them out loud.

In the paulor

One longe table with twoe greene carpetes
Five turkey worke cushinges
Fower peeces of tapestry hanginges with certain other thinges in the same roome

In the twoe bed chambers

Twoe bedsteades
Five feather beddes mattes
A payre of brasse andirons
One peece of darnex

At the stayers heade over the parlor chamber

Six ioynt stooles
An old chayre
A water pott
A stoole of ease

In the kitchinge chamber

One bedsteade mat
One liverie cubberd
A darnex curtaine and other thinges in the same roome

Andirons
Metal stands used in a fireplace to hold burning wood.

Darnex
A piece of linen cloth. This was probably made in Norwich.

Gilt plate
Gold plate.

In the kitchinge

Seaven long speetes
Seaven brasse pottes
Five kettels

Gilt plate

One bason and ure
Two flagons
Five greate bowles
Twelve spoones and one double salt with other gilt plate

Silver vessells in the closet

Twelve greate plates and fower lesser plates
One payre of candlestickes
One newe bowle with other silver plate in the same roome

Pewter belonginge to the kitchinge

Seaven saucers
Fourteene little dishes
Eyght greate dishes and other pewter

In the bearne

Cows, haifers and steers
Horses, geldinges, meares and coultes
Ewes and lambes
Poultry
Swine
Wheate
Barlie
Hay
Oates

Ure
A big jug.

Pewter
A mixture of tin and lead.

Speetes
Spits to put meat on in front of the fire.

Yeomen

Next in importance were the yeomen farmers. They owned their own small farms.

This picture shows the kitchen in a yeoman farmer's house. Today it is a museum in Warwickshire. The museum keepers used an inventory to find out what was in the room in Tudor and Stuart times.

Look at the picture again.

Can you see hooks holding other cooking pots over the fire?

One is a flat baking pan; the other is a big iron pot. The cooks boiled water in the big pot and put smaller pots inside the big one.

The plates on the shelf are made of pewter; there is a brass pot and a copper jug, but there are no gold or silver plates as there were in Sir Anthony Drury's house.

The people who lived in the house always had the fire burning. Big joints of meat were cooked on the spit in front of the fire. The meat was turned round by a pulley on the left hand side of the fireplace.

After dark the farmhouse was lit by rushlights or candles, which were made from the fat which dripped off the meat on the spit.

Herbs and sweet-smelling flowers grew in the kitchen garden. Housewives used the plants to flavour food or make medicines. In summer they mixed the flowers with rushes to put on the floor instead of having a carpet. It smelt sweet when people walked in the house.

This garden is outside the farmhouse. Look at its symmetrical shape.

Life in the Country

Husbandmen

Husbandmen were also farmers, but they were not as rich as yeomen farmers. They had money to pay rent for a small farm, but it was only big enough to provide food for their own family.

A husbandman and his son ploughing the land to get it ready to sow the seeds. 'Husbandry' is an old name for farming.

This is part of the inventory of John Flower, a husbandman who died in 1626. You can compare it with Sir Anthony's list on pages 8 and 9.

His aparell
His linen
One chest
One fether beed, one boullster and one coverlet
One kettell
Two ould sawes
One hooke
Sackes
One Sadell and one breidell
Fier wood
One cart and harness belonginge to it and plow
Fower milche cowes

Aparell
Clothes.

11

Farmworkers

The poorest people in the country did not own or rent any land. They lived in small cottages made from wooden beams, **wattle and daub,** and a roof made from thatched straw. They were sometimes called 'cottagers'.

Some were paid wages and rented a small cottage. Others were given a one-roomed cottage and a share of the crops, milk and butter instead of wages.

They all worked in the fields. This picture shows men and women out in the fields at harvest time. Men and women like these became very poor when landlords decided to change the way the land was farmed.

> **Wattle and daub**
> Woven twigs mixed with mud, horsehair and dung.

- What month of the year is it?
- Who is in charge of the workers?
- What three different jobs have to be done?
- What tools did they use to cut the corn?
- What do you think is in the pottery jug and the basket?

What do you think happened to the husbandmen when the landlords put up the rents?

What happened to the farmworkers when fields and common land was fenced in?

Did they need more workers to look after a field of sheep or to grow crops?

Life in the Country

Women

Very few women owned land in Tudor and Stuart times unless they were **widows**. You can see some of the other jobs they did, as well as working in the harvest fields, in the pictures on this page.

> **Widow**
> A woman whose husband has died.

Perhaps this woman is taking some of her spare food, eggs and butter to sell on a market stall.

There was nowhere inside the house to do the washing. It was all done by the river. Before leaving home these women made their own soap from animal fat mixed with ashes. To make it smell nice they added herbs and flowers from the garden. You can find out all about washday if you read the story in this picture. Start in the bottom right hand corner.

Find:
- the boiling water.
- the dirty clothes being beaten with wooden bats.
- the lines for hanging the clothes out to dry.

Life in the Town

Where were the towns?

Between 1500 and 1700 all the big towns in Britain increased in size. London became the largest town in the world. Norwich was the second largest town in Britain. Towns like Bristol, Exeter, Newcastle, Chester, Kings Lynn and Southampton also expanded as they were all near the **estuaries** of big rivers. Seagoing ships could bring their cargoes right into the town.

You can see what London looked like in this picture drawn in 1600. It shows both the north and south banks of the River Thames.

Find:
- the houses built very close together.
- the Tower of London on the right hand side of the north bank.
- the churches on the north bank.
- London Bridge, the most famous landmark in London, with houses and shops built on it.

There were two theatres on the South Bank of the river.

Now look at the ships on the river. They will give you an idea why London and the other towns were so busy.

The small ships with only one sail carried passengers on short journeys.

The tall ships with many different sails were seagoing ships. They carried heavy goods like coal, stone for building, sacks of wool and timber from one part of Britain to another. They also carried things to be sold in Europe and other parts of the world.

> **Estuary**
>
> The mouth of a river where it joins the sea.

Life in the Town

Along the banks of the rivers, **merchants** built warehouses to store the goods they wanted to sell abroad. The towns became overcrowded as more and more people moved in to open a warehouse or a workshop where they could make things.

Towns were not always pleasant places to live. The streets were smelly with mud and rubbish. None of the streets had drains or gutters.

> **Merchant**
> Someone who makes a living by buying and selling.

Ratcatchers were a familiar sight in the streets.
Black rats with fleas helped spread the plague, a disease which gave people a high fever and killed them. There were some cases of plague every summer.

There was no proper rubbish collection. People threw human and animal dung into the streets. People called 'rakers' were paid to throw it in the river, but most of the time they did not bother to do the job properly. Even walking in the streets was very unpleasant.

This woman wore iron rings on the bottom of her shoes when she went out in the street to lift her shoes out of the filthy mud.

There was always the risk of fire. You can read about the Great Fire of London, and the most serious outbreak of the plague, in the book *Tudor and Stuart Chronicle*.

Life in the Town

Merchants

Merchants made money from trade. Sometimes they bought raw materials, like wool, copper or gold, and sold them to craftworkers. Then they bought the finished goods back from the craftworkers and sold them to people who could not make things. Merchants owned ships so they could send goods from Britain all over the world. When the ships returned they were filled with pottery, glass, dyes, silks and spices which were then sold back in Britain.

This painting shows a merchant in his office. It was painted in 1532. He belonged to a company called the Hanse which had trade connections all over the world.

Find:
- the cloth on the table. It probably came from Turkey.
- the glass vase for the flowers. It probably came from Bohemia.
- the box of money. Merchants changed the money of one country into the money of another.
- the seals on the table. These were to mark sacks and documents with the merchant's own initials. You can see some wax seals by the back wall.
- the written papers. Perhaps these were bills or agreements about money.
- scales and weights.

Merchants' houses

Some town houses built by rich merchants in Tudor and Stuart times are still standing today.

This one belonged to John Dawtrey, a merchant in Southampton.

It is called a 'timber-framed' house. Can you see why?

We know something about the family who lived in this house from the household documents they left behind. Sir John Dawtrey was a merchant who also had a government job as a tax collector. He was rich enough to have some of the house built in brick. Each brick was made by hand. The house was his office and warehouse as well as his home. He had two wives, first Jane, then Isabel. Isabel employed eight servants to run the house.

This picture shows the inside of another merchant's house. It is in Edinburgh and the room is called the painted chamber.

A lot of wood has been used throughout the house. The furniture was all made from wood, and logs cut down from trees were burnt on the fire. What do you think happened to the forests as more and more new houses like this were built?

Shops and workshops

Anyone visiting a town in Tudor and Stuart times saw lots of small workshops with workers busy inside.

This is a shoemaker's workshop. You can see the shoes being made and being sold.

In other workshops there were:
- Clothmakers weaving cloth.
- Tailors making special clothes for wealthy people.
- Button makers making beautiful buttons from animal bones.
- Skinners and tanners turning animal skins into leather for shoes, jackets and leather buckets.
- Saddlers making saddles and bridles for horses.
- Goldsmiths and silversmiths making spoons, cups and bowls.
- Printers printing books and pictures cut on wood blocks, like the picture on this page.
- Some things, particularly food and drink, were sold from a shop window at the front.

In the street

Lots of traders had no shop or warehouse. They sold things in the street or at the market.

This man, out with his dog, sold water from his wooden barrel.

This picture shows the stallholders who have come in from the country like the woman in the picture on page 13. Most of the stalls sold food, but woollen cloth, salt, spices, pots and pans were often on sale too.

This man protected people and their belongings. He was called the bellman. People paid him to look out for thieves as there was no police force in those days.

Find:

◆ his bell and his lantern. He worked at night as well as in the day.

◆ his fierce dog.

◆ his long pole with a knife at the end.

Why do you think he has a bell?

19

William Shakespeare and the theatre

William Shakespeare was born in a market town called Stratford-upon-Avon, near the Forest of Arden in Warwickshire in 1564. His father was a farmer and also made gloves. He sent his son to a new grammar school in the town. At school Shakespeare learnt to write, do accounts, and read stories by Greek and Roman writers.

When he left school he joined a group of actors. Later he began to write plays for them. Some of Shakespeare's ideas for plays came from stories he had read at school. Some were set in a forest, like the one near his home town.

William Shakespeare moved from his home in Stratford-upon-Avon to London, and wrote plays for the London theatres.

Pedlars, like this one, travelled about selling things from a tray hung round their neck. They entertained people by telling jokes or singing songs. Shakespeare put people like this pedlar into his plays.

At first the actors performed their plays in pub yards. They were travelling players and carried all their scenery and costumes wherever they went. In 1576 two playhouses were built in Shoreditch in London. They were called the Theatre and the Curtain. The word 'theatre' comes from a Greek word which means 'a place for seeing'.

Many people did not approve of the theatre and said they should not be built in the city of London. So the next playhouses were built south of the Thames, outside the city walls.

THE SWAN THEATRE, LONDON, 1596.
Drawing in University Library, Utrecht.
Gaedertz, "Zur Kenntniss der Alt-Englischen Bühne."

This is one of the theatres called the Swan. The others were called the Rose and the Globe.

The theatres only had a roof over the back of the stage. When it rained some of the audience and the actors got wet. There was no electric light so the theatre only opened in the afternoon. Women were not allowed to be actors. All the women's parts were played by young boys. There was little scenery. The actors made their own sound effects like the noise of thunder. William Shakespeare wrote his first play when the theatres were closed because of the plague. Before he died, in 1616, he had written thirty-seven plays altogether.

Life at Court

Kings and queens

In Tudor and Stuart times most of the richest and most powerful people in the land were part of the royal court. The court was not a place, but a group of people. Wherever the king or queen went, the court went too. Can you imagine the excitement when a royal procession like this one went by?

This is a picture of Queen Elizabeth. She is being carried through the streets of London by some of her courtiers.

Find:

◆ the Queen and her attendants. How would you describe their rich, fashionable clothes?

◆ court officers. They are wearing a uniform with the Tudor Rose, the badge of the Tudor family, on their doublets.

◆ the weapons, called pikes, held by the men at the back of the picture. Why do you think they were there?

◆ the people watching the procession from windows.

Doublet

The name for a man's jacket in Tudor and Stuart times.

Life at Court

Tudor and Stuart **monarchs** paid artists to make paintings of themselves, their families and their courtiers. This painting shows Charles I on horseback. He wanted to use the painting as a kind of advertisement to show how important and powerful he was.

Find:

- the royal crown. It is not on the King's head, but it is still in the painting.
- the shield painted with the royal coat of arms.
- the King's armour and lace collar. Do you think Charles chose these clothes for his picture? They show him both as a brave soldier and as a leader of fashion.
- his long curly hair. This was the fashionable hairstyle for men at the time.
- the background to the picture. Do you think it is a real place?
- the riding teacher in the front.

How does the artist make us look at the King more than at the riding teacher?

Why do you think the King liked this artist, Anthony van Dyck, so much?

Monarch
King or queen.

Coat of arms
'Arms' is an old word for badge.

Courtiers

Some members of the court gave advice to the monarch. Others had jobs as members of the Royal Household. Some were the monarch's favourite friends.

This carving is at Hatfield House where Queen Elizabeth was living when she became Queen. It shows her surrounded by her courtiers.

- How many courtiers can you see?
- Are most of them men or women?
- How are they dressed for life at court?
- How has the artist managed to show us that the most important person at court was the Queen?

Members of the court were not paid, but received free food and drink in return for the advice or service they gave. Everyone had a daily allowance of beer or wine. Courtiers still had a lot of expenses which they had to pay themselves.

Some courtiers had jobs as Lords or Ladies in Waiting, doctors, chaplains, grooms or pages. Others were Masters of the Horse and Hounds, Masters and Mistresses of the Wardrobe or Masters of the Revels. Courtiers brought their own servants to court too. They worked in the kitchens and laundry or did jobs outside the palace. Sometimes as many as 500 people lived at court.

The young man in this picture is dressed in the latest fashion like many of the people at court.

His clothes were expensive and made of silk, satin, lace and velvet. They were hand-sewn with beads and silk flowers. Do you think he is trying to look like a fashion model in this picture?

Life at Court

The court was also part of the government. In Tudor and Stuart times the monarch ruled the country with the help of the Privy Council and Parliament. Some of the most important courtiers were in the Privy Council. You can read more about Parliament and what happened when it disagreed with the ruling of the court in the book *Tudor and Stuart Chronicle*.

This is William Cecil who was Queen Elizabeth's chief adviser for forty years. He often went to Parliament, and was a member of the House of Commons.

Find:

- his white stick. Only someone with an important position in the royal household was allowed to carry this.
- his black clothes trimmed with gold brocade. Only a minister was allowed to wear a uniform like this.
- the documents on the table. They are put there to show he was allowed to look at important papers of state.

Both the fashionable young man on page 24 and William Cecil were members of the court. Their portraits show two different points of view about the life of a courtier.

Life at Court

Royal palaces

Tudor and Stuart monarchs often moved from one royal palace to another. You can see some of their palaces on this page and read about some of the events which happened in them in *Tudor and Stuart Chronicle*.

This palace is called Hampton Court Palace. It was built by Cardinal Wolsey, one of Henry VIII's advisers, who gave it to the King as a present.

The palace was built of red brick beside the River Thames, a short boat journey away from London. All the bricks were made by hand. This shows that someone very wealthy built the palace. The Great Gatehouse was built to impress people when they first arrived.

King Henry VIII also had one of the first tennis courts in England built at Hampton Court. It was for a game called 'Real Tennis'.

In Scotland, Holyrood House was the royal palace. Mary, Queen of Scots lived there with her own court. This is Mary's bedroom. Some of her furniture has been collected and put on display here.

Life at Court

At Christmas, when it was someone's birthday or when someone was married, the Master of Revels organised entertainment at court. Musicians, actors, jesters, tumblers and clowns were all invited to perform. Many people joined in singing madrigals and dancing as well as performing in **masques**.

> **Masques**
>
> Plays put on at court. The actors, often courtiers, disguised themselves by wearing masks.

Queen Elizabeth was a very good dancer. This dance is called the 'volta'. Other dances were the 'pavan' (stately and slow) and the 'galliard' (quick and jolly).

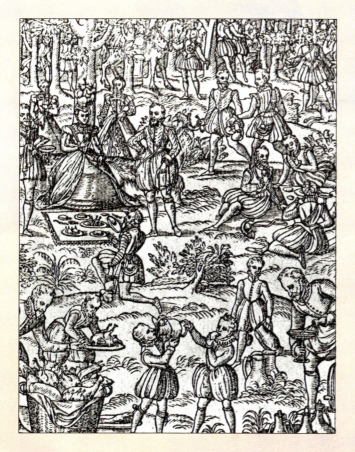

In summer the court entertained themselves in the country. Some people now think that some of their sports, like hunting hares and wild deer and trapping birds were very cruel, but this hunting party look as if they are having a good time.

Find:
- the Queen, her ladies-in-waiting and other courtiers.
- the Queen's horse.
- picnic cloths spread out on the ground.
- servants taking the food from a big basket. What are they having to eat?
- servants filling a cup and some jugs with beer from the barrels.
- a man with a hunting horn round his waist.

Religious Life

Going to church

In Tudor and Stuart times, everyone had to go to church on Sunday or pay a fine of money.

When Henry VII was king, everyone belonged to the Roman Catholic Church. They obeyed the Pope who lived in Rome. But other monarchs wanted to change the way things were done. Any changes were announced by priests from the **pulpit**.

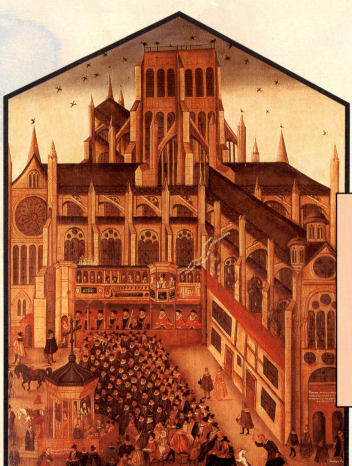

Pulpit

The place where a priest stood so that everyone could see him.

This picture shows a priest in the pulpit outside St Paul's Church in London in the time of King James I.

Find:
- the priest in the pulpit.
- the Mayor and aldermen of London.
- King James I of England, and VI of Scotland.
- ordinary people listening to the priest. Most people did what the priests told them to do. If what was done in church changed, most just accepted it, but some people found this more difficult.

Aldermen

Men chosen to help the Mayor run London.

Religious Life

The first monarch to make a change was King Henry VIII. In 1534 he made himself head of the Church in England. You can read about it in the book called *Tudor and Stuart Chronicle*.

When he had done this he ordered that all the land and property which once belonged to the Pope in Rome should be taken over. Monasteries, for monks, and nunneries, for nuns, were closed.

As well as praying in church, monks and nuns ran farms, schools and hospitals. They also gave food and shelter to travellers and the poor.

Some people were pleased when the monasteries and nunneries were closed down. The money and land was given away, some to the King's supporters. They used it to build themselves new country houses.

Other people were not pleased. They included the monks and nuns themselves and the people they had helped. They still wanted to be part of the Roman Catholic Church with the Pope as head of the Church.

Religious Life

Roman Catholics

Some families decided to stay as members of the Roman Catholic Church even when they knew this was against the law. The only time they could admit that they were Roman Catholics was in the five years when Queen Mary was on the throne, from 1553 to 1558. The rest of the time they had to say **mass** in secret.

This picture shows Roman Catholic women praying together in private. If they were discovered they were put in prison. Do you think they were brave or foolish?

> **Mass**
> The most important set of prayers in the Roman Catholic Church.

There were plots to put a Catholic monarch on the throne again in the reigns of both Queen Elizabeth and King James. The Gunpowder Plot, which you can read about in *Tudor and Stuart Chronicle*, was one of these.

Soldiers were sometimes sent out to arrest any priests found holding a Catholic service because they thought that they might be plotting rather than praying.

This picture shows a hiding place under the floor boards in a country house belonging to a Catholic family. If soldiers came, the priest quickly got inside.

Religious Life

Protestants

For many people breaking away from the Pope in Rome was not enough. They began to protest about what they thought was wrong about the Church and its services. These protesters called themselves 'Protestants'.

- They wanted a prayer book written in English, not Latin.
- They wanted services to be simple and easy to understand.
- They wanted to get rid of the pictures and statues which Catholics liked to have in their churches.
- They thought that priests should be allowed to marry and have children.

King Edward VI was a Protestant and ordered these things to be changed. But his sister Mary was a Catholic. When she became Queen she ordered all Protestants to be burnt as **heretics**.

> **Heretic**
> Someone who refused to support the official church.

This picture shows a Protestant preacher being burnt alive. Two hundred and eighty Protestants were burnt like this in less than four years in Mary's reign. The burnings went on all over Britain.

Religious Life

Puritans

During the reign of Queen Elizabeth many people began to support the religious ideas of the Puritans. Puritan comes from the word 'pure'. Puritans thought that priests had too much power. They believed that anyone could get directly in touch with God by reading the **Bible** and living a pure, simple life.

> **Bible**
> The book of Christian holy writings.

The Puritans also thought that churches should not be run by bishops appointed by the monarch, but by ministers elected by church members.

Puritans dressed in grey, black, brown and white rather than in bright colours. They disapproved of people playing sports and games on Sundays.

This painting shows a Puritan family. The boy on the right hand side has opened the Bible. His father is going to write down some texts for the family to study.

What do you think about:
- the colour of their clothes.
- the father's tall hat.
- the plain linen caps worn by the mother and the girls.

You can read more about the Puritans in *Tudor and Stuart Chronicle*.

> **Texts**
> Verses in the Bible.

Religious Life

Witchcraft

Some things that happened could not be explained by reading the Bible or praying, particularly as people in Tudor and Stuart times did not know as much science as we know today. They thought that unexpected bad luck, crops which did not grow, sudden illness or death, even the milk turning sour in the hot sun, happened because of magic. Some men and women were even accused of 'bewitching' people.

Between 1644 and 1647 Matthew Hopkins was asked to hunt out witches. He was paid a big sum of money for every woman he could bring before the court to be tried as a witch.

This is the front page of his book *The Discovery of Witches*.

Find:

- the Lord Chief Justice, Sir John Holt.
- the woman accused of being a witch.
- some of the animals she is supposed to use to help her perform her witchcraft.

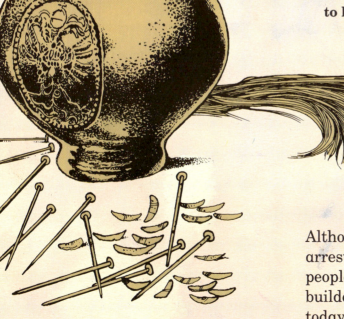

Although many women were unfairly arrested and tortured as 'witches', lots of people really believed in witchcraft. When builders repair old Tudor and Stuart houses today they often find magic charms, like these, buried in the walls. They were put there to keep the witches away.

Life in the Army

In Tudor and Stuart times there was no regular army as we have now. Every town or village in the land had to be ready to send some soldiers, with their weapons, if they were told to do so by the king or queen.

An artist drew this picture to show an English army on the march in Ireland.

Find:

- the five horsemen leading the army.
- the flags held by a group called the standard bearers. If fighting began, soldiers kept together by gathering under the flags.
- the soldier with a bugle. When it was blown, the rest of the soldiers knew they had to start fighting.
- the head armour worn by every soldier.
- the body armour worn by some groups.
- four different sorts of weapon, daggers, swords, pikes and muskets.

Which side do you think the artist who drew this picture supported? The Irish or the English?

Musket

A firearm with gunpowder inside.

Life in the Army

English armies were often sent to Ireland. The English said that Ireland was really part of Britain and that the Irish people were rebels who had to be controlled by force.

The Irish, who were Roman Catholics, said the English were foreigners who wanted to steal Irish land and make them all into Protestants.

All men between the ages of sixteen and sixty had to attend regular drill and weapon practice. They were called the local 'militia' and trained to be members of the **infantry**.

> **Infantry**
>
> Foot soldiers.

This picture comes from a book printed in 1595. It shows some soldiers drilling with pikes.

Look how they have to move their legs and bodies as well as the weapons in their arms.

This picture shows a cannon being fired. As it was such a heavy gun it was loaded on a platform on wheels, but they were not much use on a muddy battlefield.

Civil War soldiers

Many more men became soldiers during the Civil War between 1642 and 1646. You can read more about the battles they fought in the book *Tudor and Stuart Chronicle*.

This picture shows you what an ordinary foot soldier looked like.

Find his:

- leather trousers, jacket and boots.
- iron helmet. When he was not fighting he wore a felt hat.
- sword.
- musket with a piece of string for lighting the gunpowder.
- belt with a pocket purse.
- metal box. He kept the gunpowder in this so that it would not catch fire by accident.

The soldiers were not well paid. At night they were lucky if someone gave them a bed in a cottage or farm. Usually they had to sleep under hedges or in barns. Women and children also travelled with the army. The women prepared food, gave medicine and washed the clothes.

The two sides in the Civil War gave each other rude names. Parliament's soldiers called the king's soldiers 'Cavaliers'. This came from the Spanish word 'cabellero', meaning 'soldier on horseback'. The English did not like the Spanish.

The Royalists, who supported the King, called the other side 'Roundheads'. This was a rude name, usually only given to rough young men who cut their hair short. It was the fashion for all men to have long hair in Tudor and Stuart times.

The New Model Army

The Roundheads were the first people to make changes when they reorganised their soldiers into a new 'model' army.

This museum display shows weapons and armour used in the Civil War.

The New Model Army was more like the army we have today. The soldiers, particularly the **cavalry**, were all trained properly. They were given uniforms and equipment and were paid a proper wage. They were organised into divisions or teams, and were put under the command of a strong leader.

Cavalry
Soldiers on horseback.

The infantry were not as important as the cavalry in the New Model Army, but they had particular jobs to do. The pikemen slowed down the enemy. This gave the musketeer time to load his musket with gunpowder.

The New Model Army won the first battle it ever fought. This was at Naseby in Northamptonshire. You can see a picture of the battle and read more about it in the book called *Tudor and Stuart Chronicle*.

Life at Sea

The *Mary Rose*

In Tudor and Stuart times, shipbuilders learnt how to make bigger and better ships. The ships were used to fight battles at sea, to explore new places and to take traders and settlers to countries where British people had not been before.

One Tudor ship we know a lot about was the *Mary Rose*, a new warship which sank in 1545 before it had ever taken part in a battle at sea.

This is a part of the *Mary Rose* archaeologists rescued from the bottom of the sea. From it they found out:

- the ship was built of wood.
- it was about thirty-two metres long and the height of a four storey building.
- there were three decks and a 'hold'. This was the part of the ship that went under the water. Heavy things stored there helped the ship keep its balance.
- a rudder at the back of the ship helped steer it in the right direction.
- one of the decks was a gun deck.

Life at Sea

People alive at the time also wrote about the *Mary Rose* before she sank. From their account we know that the ship had room for 120 sailors, 251 soldiers, twenty gunners, two pilots, five trumpeters and thirty-six servants. The officers had better cabins than the ordinary seamen, with more expensive furnishing.

More than 17,000 objects from the ship have been found. Here are some of them.

A comb, a whistle, some coins and a rosary, used by Catholics when they said their prayers.

Dividers for measuring distance on a map.

Tools, to repair the ship in time of war.

The ship's bell, for calling all the sailors on deck.

This picture shows what the *Mary Rose* probably looked like. It is a drawing of a famous warship, the flagship of the Armada, the *Ark Royal* built in 1587. Think about what it was like for the sailors who sailed it.

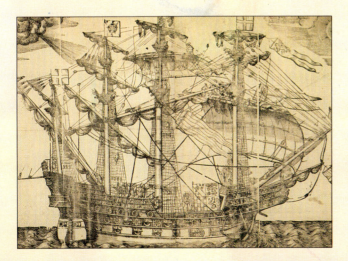

You can see another Tudor warship, the *Great Harry*, in the book *Tudor and Stuart Chronicle*.

Find:

- four vertical masts. Sailors had to climb to the crow's nest at the top to keep a lookout for other warships.
- horizontal masts, which hold the sails. Some of them have been rolled up for the time being.
- ropes, called 'rigging'. Sailors had to climb up and down these to open and close the sails.
- the gun deck. During a battle, sailors had to keep filling up the cannon with gunpowder.

Exploration

Some ships were built not for war, but for exploring and crossing oceans. The captains of these ships, sometimes called 'sea dogs', wanted to find a sea route to the east, where they could buy spices, silks and precious stones. They had also heard stories of Spanish treasure ships full of gold and silver from the mines in South America.

This is a picture of an English ship called the *Desire* in a storm in the Straits of Magellan. What do you think it was like to be a sailor on a ship like this?

You can read about some of the jobs that had to be done on board a ship like the *Desire* in the book called *Explorations*, but no one knows for certain what it was like to be a sailor. Try to imagine their point of view:

- No one knew how long the journey would take.
- Food had to be stored on board for a long voyage. Some of this went bad. Some live animals were taken on board and killed for food.
- Drinking water was often in short supply.
- They had few maps and no clocks, and relied a great deal on the stars. Some new mathematical instruments, like the compass, were available.
- The ship often ran into bad weather. Sailors had to put up the right sails according to the direction of the wind.
- It was cold and wet for most of the journey. Many sailors died from accidents or food poisoning.

This picture shows what it was like when the sailors on the *Desire* arrived in Guam, a tropical island in the Pacific Ocean.

Find:

- the *Desire* and its sister ship the *Content*.
- the captain of the ship, Thomas Cavendish, standing at the front of the *Desire*.
- the English sailors in their small boat beside the *Desire*. Why were they firing guns?
- the people who lived in Guam. What is different about their boats?
- the fresh fruit they are taking out to the English sailors. Why do you think they wanted this?
- the people holding up fish.

One sea captain, John Hawkins, was a **slave** trader. He sailed from Plymouth, in Devon, to the west coast of Africa. There he took African prisoners and sold them to the Spanish in return for gold. Some of the slaves were made to work growing cotton or tobacco in America. Others were sold as servants to rich families in Spain, Portugal and Britain. You can see one of them in the left hand side of the picture on page 7.

> **Slave**
>
> **A human being with no rights of their own. They could be sold by their owner to someone else.**

A New Life

India

Some people in Tudor and Stuart times left their homes in Britain to make a new life in another part of the world.

The first English traveller to arrive in India may have been Thomas Stevens, a Catholic priest. This Indian painting shows the court of the Emperor Akbar, which he visited in 1579.

Find:

- Akbar on his throne. He was head of the Mughal Empire which covered most of India, Pakistan and Bangladesh.
- members of his court. They are pouring coloured water over his head.
- the peacocks in the garden outside the palace. The Mughals loved gardens.
- the bright clothes worn by all the people in the painting. These were made from the best Indian silks and cotton cloth.
- the big fan held by one of the men on the ground.
- huntsmen and warriors with arrows, a gun and swords. Two of the men have hunting birds on their arms.

Which things are the same as a British court, and which things are different?

A New Life

Six years after his visit, English merchants began arriving in India. In 1600 they formed themselves into a company called the East India Company and sent their ships to Surat where they built a British trading post. When more traders arrived to live in India they put up warehouses in Madras and Bengal.

This picture shows an English merchant from the point of view of an Indian artist. What things about his appearance has the artist noticed? What details have been left out?

The Mughal Indians made some of the best cloth in the world. They used silk and cotton which could not be produced in Britain. The British traders wanted to buy cloth and many other things in India which they could sell in Europe, such as: pepper, spices, a drug called opium, a blue dye called indigo and some of the beautiful craftwork made at Akbar's court.

More and more British merchants wanted to join the East India Company.

In 1614, King James I sent an **ambassador** called Sir Thomas Roe to live in India and represent him.

> **Ambassador**
> Someone representing his government in another country.

A New Life

America

In 1585 one of Queen Elizabeth's favourite courtiers, Sir Walter Raleigh, persuaded some friends to put up the money for ships to take British settlers to the east coast of America. They called the place where they arrived 'Virginia'. One of the people who made the journey was an artist called John White, who painted the people already living there. The Europeans called them 'Indians' because the first people to sail from Europe to America thought they had arrived in India, but each **tribe** had its own name.

This is one of John White's paintings of a Powhatan Indian he met.

Find:

- the painted decoration on the man's body. John White wrote that the Powhatan did this when they were going hunting or feasting.
- the bow and arrow case.
- the clothes made of leather.
- the bison's tail. This showed what a good hunter he was. The bison provided them with meat, milk and leather.

Tribe

A group of families living together in one area.

A New Life

This is a picture map drawn for John Smith, the first British governor of Virginia, who arrived there in 1607.

Find:

- the coat of arms of King James I of England, and VI of Scotland. The British called the town they built there 'Jamestown'.
- a British ship arriving at Cape Charles. Who do you think this was named after?
- the scale measuring leagues. A league was about five kilometres.
- the rivers for travelling inland.
- the villages and hunting grounds of the Powhatans. It was their land before the British arrived. You can see a hunter on the right hand side of the picture.

The small picture in the left hand corner of the map tells a story about John Smith. One day he was taken prisoner and Chief Powhatan, who you can see in the picture, said he should be executed because the British had taken the Powhatan's best land.

The Chief had a daughter called Pocahontas who had made friends with the settlers. She asked her father to make peace with the British as she wanted to marry one of them. Chief Powhatan agreed and let John Smith go free.

Pocahontas travelled to England where she lived with her husband until she died.

The *Mayflower*

One story that is certainly true is about families, usually called the 'Pilgrim Fathers', who crossed the Atlantic Ocean in 1620 in this ship, called the *Mayflower*. They were Puritans who had not been been allowed to hold the church services they wanted in England.

There were about 102 passengers on the *Mayflower*. They had all decided that they would make a new life in America and never go back to Britain. They had to take everything they needed for their new life with them, including tools to build homes and start a farm.

The journey lasted 66 days and the weather at sea was very stormy. A new baby was born during the voyage. His mother called him Oceanus. Why do you think she chose this name?

When the Puritans arrived in America, it was already nearly winter. They had to cut down trees, and build themselves some homes, with the tools they had brought on the ship.

This a model of the *Mayflower* which was about thirty metres long and seven metres wide. If you mark out these measurements outside you will see that it was not a very big ship.

A New Life

Instead of fighting each other, the Puritans and the Indians made friends. The Indians gave them some corn and showed them that if they saved some of the seed, they could plant it in the spring and have another crop the next year.

This painting was not painted when the Puritans first arrived, but about 200 years later. It is an artist's idea about one of the first families from the *Mayflower*.

We know that many Puritan families like this one travelled across the Atlantic for a new life. Many of them gave their new towns the same names as the towns they left behind. The *Mayflower* families called their town 'Plymouth', after the port they sailed from in Britain.

Look at a map of the United States and at the names of towns near the east coast. Perhaps you will find some places with the same names as British towns. You could start with New York!

A New Life

The first European settlers found plants growing in America that they had not seen in Europe. Some of them were good to eat like the Indian corn, which we call sweet corn. Others included the potato and the tomato.

This picture shows that another plant that only grew in America had been brought back to Britain. What they did not know then was that smoking was very bad for their health.

If someone asked you to put a date on this picture, what would you say?

Was it at the beginning of Tudor and Stuart times or somewhere near the end?

This is the sort of puzzle people often have to do with evidence in history.